Why do we remember?

THE GREAT FIRE OF LONDON

Izzi Howell

W
FRANKLIN WATTS
LONDON•SYDNEY

Franklin Watts

First published in Great Britain in 2016 by The Watts Publishing Group

Copyright © The Watts Publishing Group, 2016

Produced for Franklin Watts by
White-Thomson Publishing Ltd
www.wtpub.co.uk

ISBN: 978 1 4451 4824 3

Credits
Series Editor: Izzi Howell
Series Designer: Rocket Design (East Anglia) Ltd

The publisher would like to thank the following for permission to reproduce their pictures: Alamy/North Wind Picture Archives pp6-7 (bottom); Alamy/Walker Art Library 8; Alamy/Mary Evans Picture Library 24; Alamy/ The National Trust Photolibrary 25; Bridgeman Images/Bonhams, London, UK 24; Corbis/Heritage Images pp4-5; Corbis/Michael Nicholson 20; iStock/aurielaki (title page and cover); iStock/Claudiad 23; iStock/ duncan1890 21; iStock/HultonArchive 2 and 16; iStock/Lauri Patterson 10; iStock/JOHN GOMEZ 28 (right); iStock/Pauws99 9; Museum of London 15 (bottom); Shutterstock/chrisdorney 13, 27; Shutterstock/ Claudio Divizia 28 (right); Shutterstock/Diana Taliun 17 (bottom); Shutterstock/Everett Historical 7 (top), 26; Shutterstock/Martina I. Meyer 17 (top); Shutterstock/Neil Mitchell 29; Shutterstock/worker 15 (top); Wellcome Library, London/R. Nanteuil 19; Wikimedia/H.B. Wheatley (title page, cover and 12); Wikimedia 11. All design elements from Shutterstock.

Every attempt has been made to clear copyright. Should there be any inadvertent omission please apply to the publisher for rectification.

Printed in China

MIX
Paper from
responsible sources
FSC® C104740
FSC
www.fsc.org

Franklin Watts
An imprint of
Hachette Children's Group
Part of The Watts Publishing Group
Carmelite House
50 Victoria Embankment
London EC4Y 0DZ

An Hachette UK Company
www.hachette.co.uk
www.franklinwatts.co.uk

Words in **bold** can be found in the glossary on p30.

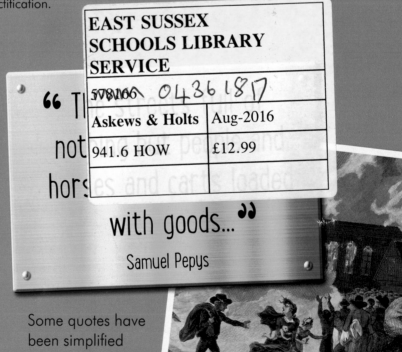

" Th... not... hors... with goods... "

Samuel Pepys

Some quotes have been simplified and revised with modern spelling.

CONTENTS

LONDON'S <u>BURNING</u>

In September 1666, a huge fire burnt for five days in the centre of London. Many houses and buildings were **destroyed** by the flames. This fire is known as the Great Fire of London.

After the Great Fire, new buildings were built in the centre of London. It became a safer and cleaner city. We remember the Great Fire because it changed the **landscape** of London forever.

▼ The huge flames of the Great Fire of London reached high into the sky.

HOW do we know?

Many years after the fire, the song 'London's Burning' became a way to help children remember the story of the Great Fire of London.

LONDON'S BURNING

London's burning, London's burning,
Fetch the engines, fetch the engines,
Fire, fire! Fire, fire!
Pour on water, pour on water.

WHAT do you think?

Can you think of any other songs that help you remember things?

▲ Although this song mentions engines, people didn't have anything like today's fire engines to fight the Great Fire. They had to use buckets of water and pumps that squirted water at the fire.

A PLAGUE ON YOU!

In the **17th century**, London was a busy city with many people living close together on both sides of the River Thames. The streets were narrow and dirty, filled with rubbish and rats.

HOW do we know?

Drawings of London from before the Great Fire show us that buildings in the city were built close together.

▼ Many ships and boats sailed along the River Thames in the 17th century.

St Paul's Cathedral

River Thames

In 1665, many people in London became sick with a terrible disease called the **plague**. Nobody knew how to treat the plague. It **spread** quickly through the dirty, crowded city centre, killing over 100,000 people.

◄ People with the plague had headaches, fevers and red lumps all over their bodies.

London Bridge

Tower of London

FIND OUT FOR YOURSELF
How many bridges crossed the River Thames in London in 1666?

MADE OF <u>WOOD</u>

Before the Great Fire, most buildings in London were made from wood. The top floors of buildings often stuck out over the street so that there was more room inside.

These wooden buildings often caught on fire as people used candles to light their homes and places of work. Women also cooked meals on open fires inside their homes.

▶ Many buildings in 17th century London had shops on the ground floor.

HOW do we know?

You can visit wooden buildings in London that survived the fire, such as Staple Inn.

▼ Staple Inn on High Holborn in London.

WHAT do you think?

How do we light modern homes? How do people usually cook their food today?

A SPARK IN THE DARK

At 1 a.m. on 2 September 1666, a fire started in a bakery in Pudding Lane, London. After a hot summer, the wooden buildings near the bakery were very dry. They quickly caught on fire as well.

A strong wind was blowing that night. It helped to spread the fire to other parts of London. By the morning, the fire was out of control!

► The bakery in Pudding Lane baked bread in an oven heated by fire.

HOW do we know?

A newspaper called the *London Gazette* printed an article about the fire on 10 September 1666. From this article, we know the date, the time and the street where the fire started.

'At one o' clock in the morning, there happened to break out a ... fire in Pudding Lane'

WHAT do you think?

Today, many people still find out about important events from newspapers. Can you think of some other ways that we learn about important events?

THE LONDON GAZET

Published by Authority.

From **Monday**, Septemb 3, to **Monday**, Septemp 10, 1666.

Whitehall, Sept. 8.

THE ordinary course of this paper having been interrupted by a sad and lamentable accident of Fire lately hapned in the City of *London*: it hath been thought fit for satisfying the minds of so many of His Majesties good Subjects who must needs be concerned for the Issue of so great an accident, to give this short, but true Accompt of it.

On the second instant, at one of the clock in the Morning, there hapned to break out, a sad in deplorable Fire in *Pudding-lane*, neer *New Fish-street*, which falling out at that hour of the night, and in a quarter of the Town so close built with wooden pitched houses spread itself so far before day, and with such distraction to the inhabitants and Neighbours, that care was not taken for the timely preventing the further diffusion of it, by pulling down houses, as ought to have been; so that this lamentable Fire in a short time became too big to be mastred by any Engines or working neer it. It fell out most unhappily too, That a violent wind fomented and kept it burning all ... and the following spreading itself ... et and downwards from ...ater-side, as far as the *Three* ...

... in all parts about it, distracted by ...ss of it, and their particular care to carry ...ir Goods, many attempts were made to ... the spreading of it by pulling down ...es, and making great Intervals, but all in vain, the Fire seizing upon the Timber and Rubbish, and so continuing it set even through those spaces, and raging in a bright flame all Monday and Teusday, not withstanding His Majesties own, and His Royal Highness's indefatigable and personal pains to apply all possible remedies to prevent it, calling upon and helping the people with their Guards; and a great number of Nobility and Gentry unwearidly assisting therein, for which they were requited with a thousand blessings from the poor distressed people. By the favour of God the Wind slackened a little on Teusday night & the Flames meeting with brick buildings at the *Temple*, by little and little it was observed to lose its force on that side, so that on We... morning we began to hope well o... Highness never despairing or ... sonal care wrought so wel... some parts by the Lords ... behind is that a stop w...

Church, neer *Holborn-bridge, Pie-corner*, *Cripple-gate*, neer the lower end of *Co...* at the end of *Basin-hall-street* by the *Po...* upper end of *Bishopsgate-street* and ... *street*, at the *Standard* in *Cornhill* at the *Fenchurch street*, neer *Cloth-workers Hall* i... *lane*, at the middle of *Mark-lane*, and at ... dock.

On Thursday by the blessing of G... wholly beat down and extinguished. ... that Evening it unhappily burst out again... the *Temple*, by the falling of some spa... supposed) upon a Pile of Wooden build... his Royal Highness who watched there th... night in Person, by the great labours and ... used, and especially by applying Powde... up the Houses about it, before day most ... mastered it.

Divers Strangers, Dutch and Frenc... during the fire, apprehended, upon suspic... they contributed mischievously to it, who... imprisoned, and Informations prepared to... severe inquisition here upon by my Lo... Justice *Keeling*, assisted by some of the ... the Privy Council; and some principal M... of the City, notwithstanding which suspici... manner of the burning all along in a Train,... blowen forwards in all its way by strong... make us conclude the whole was an effec... unhappy chance, or to speak better, the... hand of God upon us for our sins, shewing... terrour of his Judgement in thus raising the... and immediately after his miraculous and ne... be acknowledged Mercy, in putting a stop... when we were in the last despair, and th... attempts for quenching it however industr... pursued seemed insufficient. His Majesty ... sat hourly in Council, and ever since hath ... tinued making rounds about the City in all pa... it where the danger and mischief was greates... this morning that he hath sent his Grace the ... of *Albemarle*, whom he hath called for to s... him in this great occasion, to put his happy ... successful hand to the finishing this memor... deliverance.

About the *Tower* the seasonable orders g... for plucking down the Houses to secure the M... zines of Powder was more especially success... that part being up the Wind, notwithstand... ...ich it came almost to the very Gates of it. ... this early provision the general Stores ...ged in the *Tower* were entirely save... ...ve further this intimate cause to g... ... that the Fire did not happen whe...

FIND OUT FOR YOURSELF
Who owned the bakery where the fire started?

DEAR DIARY

A man called Samuel Pepys (1633–1703) lived in London at the time of the fire. He worked for the **government** and was friends with important people, including the king of England, Charles II (1630–1685). Pepys kept a diary about what he saw and did in London.

On the first day of the fire, we know that Pepys watched the flames from the Tower of London because he wrote about it in his diary.

▶ We have learned a lot of information about London in the 17th century from Pepys' diary.

66 I ...walked to the Tower ...and there I did see the houses at that end of the bridge all on fire. 99

Samuel Pepys

HOW do we know?

You can read Pepys' **eyewitness** account of the Great Fire in his diary. We can learn a lot about the Great Fire from Pepys, as he wrote in his diary on every day of the fire.

WHAT do you think?

Have you been an eyewitness to any important events? Why are eyewitness accounts important?

FIND OUT FOR YOURSELF
When did Pepys start writing his diary?

◀ Pepys climbed up one of the towers at the Tower of London to see the fire better.

ENTRY TO THE TRAITORS GATE

FIGHTING THE FLAMES

There was no fire brigade in 1666. Ordinary people had to fight the fire themselves, using buckets of water and water pumps to put out the flames. Even the king and his brother helped to carry water.

To stop the wind spreading the flames from house to house, King Charles II ordered people to pull down buildings that were in the path of the fire. They used **fire hooks** to tear down wooden walls and blew up houses with **gunpowder**.

▲ This drawing from the 1600s shows how people put out fires at the time of the Great Fire of London.

HOW do we know?

When **archaeologists** dug up the ground near Pudding Lane, they found buckets left behind after the Great Fire of London.

▲ Archaeologists dig for historical remains in London.

◀ A leather bucket from the 1600s.

WHAT do you think?

Why was it difficult for people to fight the fire with buckets of water? Why is it easier for fire fighters to put out fires today?

PRECIOUS POSSESSIONS

The fire spread too quickly for people to save their houses. Instead, they carried away their most **valuable possessions**, such as books and jewellery, and left their houses to burn.

> 66 The streets full of nothing but people and horses and carts loaded with goods... 99
>
> Samuel Pepys

▼ These people are escaping from the fire with their possessions in sacks.

Some people brought their possessions down to the river, and left them on ships far from the **shore**. Other people used carts to carry their things to other parts of London. Pepys even buried some items in his garden!

▼ Pepys took his money and silver plates away on a cart, and buried his valuable cheese.

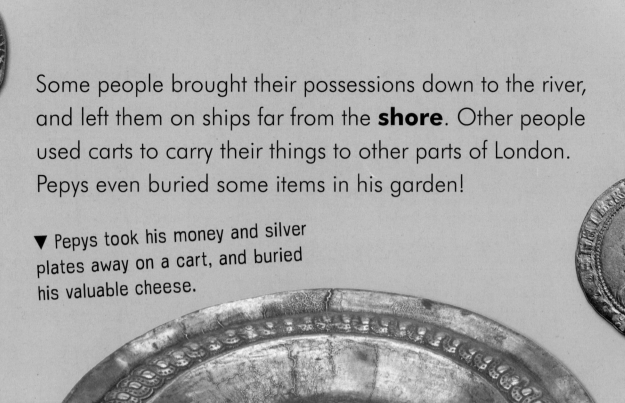

<u>WHAT</u> do you think?

What would you save from your house in a fire?

FIND OUT FOR YOURSELF
What type of cheese did Pepys save from the fire?

ASHES AND EMBERS

People were worried that the fire would spread across London Bridge, and carry the flames from the north side to the south side of London. Luckily, on 5 September, the wind dropped and the fire started to go out.

By the morning of 6 September, the fire had died out. The centre of London was filled with burnt **rubble** and **ashes**. For several days after the fire, the ground was too hot to walk on.

▼ After the fire, glowing hot pieces of wood called embers covered the city.

HOW do we know?

Another writer, John Evelyn (1620–1706), kept a diary through the Great Fire of London. He wrote about what it was like to walk through London after the fire.

▼ John Evelyn

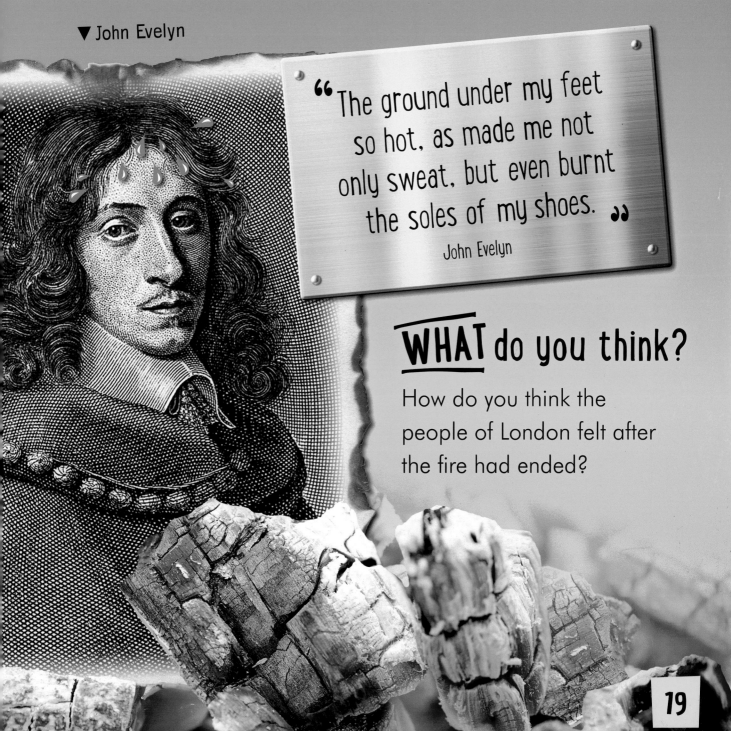

" The ground under my feet so hot, as made me not only sweat, but even burnt the soles of my shoes. "

John Evelyn

WHAT do you think?

How do you think the people of London felt after the fire had ended?

19

BURNT DOWN

After the Great Fire of London, the centre of London was almost empty. The flames had destroyed around 13,000 buildings and more than 80 churches. The dirty, crowded neighbourhoods were gone.

Records from the time say that fewer than ten people died in the fire. However, we don't know exactly how many people died, as the deaths of poor people weren't always written down.

▼ The fire was so hot that the metal roof of St Paul's Cathedral melted!

Look, it's melting!

<u>HOW</u> do we know?

We can look at maps drawn after the fire to see which parts of London burnt down.

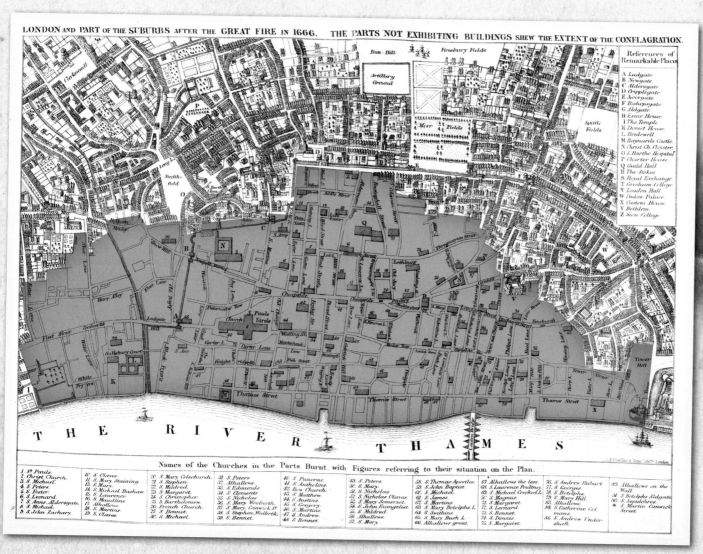

▲ The area shaded orange shows how far the Great Fire spread.

HUNTING FOR A <u>HOME</u>

Over 100,000 people lost their homes in the Great Fire of London. During the fire, many people escaped to the fields outside of London, where they camped in tents. After the fire, King Charles II visited the homeless people and brought them bread to eat.

▼ This painting shows a group of people camping in Highgate Fields while the Great Fire of London burns in the distance.

While London was being rebuilt, some people went to live in areas of London that hadn't been **damaged**. Other people moved to different cities, or even other countries.

WHAT do you think?

Some people become homeless today because of wars or **natural disasters**. How would you feel if you became homeless?

▶ These people from Iraq have lost their homes because of a war. They are living in a camp.

A NEW LONDON

King Charles II knew that it was important to rebuild London properly. He worked with **architects** to redesign the city so that it wouldn't catch fire so easily again.

The new buildings had to be made from brick or stone. They were built further apart so that it would be difficult for fires and diseases, such as the plague, to spread from house to house.

▶ Many architects presented their ideas about how to rebuild London to the king.

HOW do we know?

We can read the rules that King Charles made about new buildings.

> "No man shall build any house or building, great or small, from anything other than brick or stone."
>
> King Charles II

▶ King Charles II

WHAT do you think?

Why are stone buildings safer than wooden buildings? What materials are most modern houses made from?

WREN REBUILDS

Christopher Wren (1632–1723) was a **talented** architect. He designed many buildings that were built in London after the fire. He planned how to rebuild 52 damaged churches in London, including the massive St Paul's Cathedral.

Work on rebuilding St Paul's Cathedral began in 1675. It took 36 years to finish, by which time Christopher Wren was 79 years old!

▶ Christopher Wren

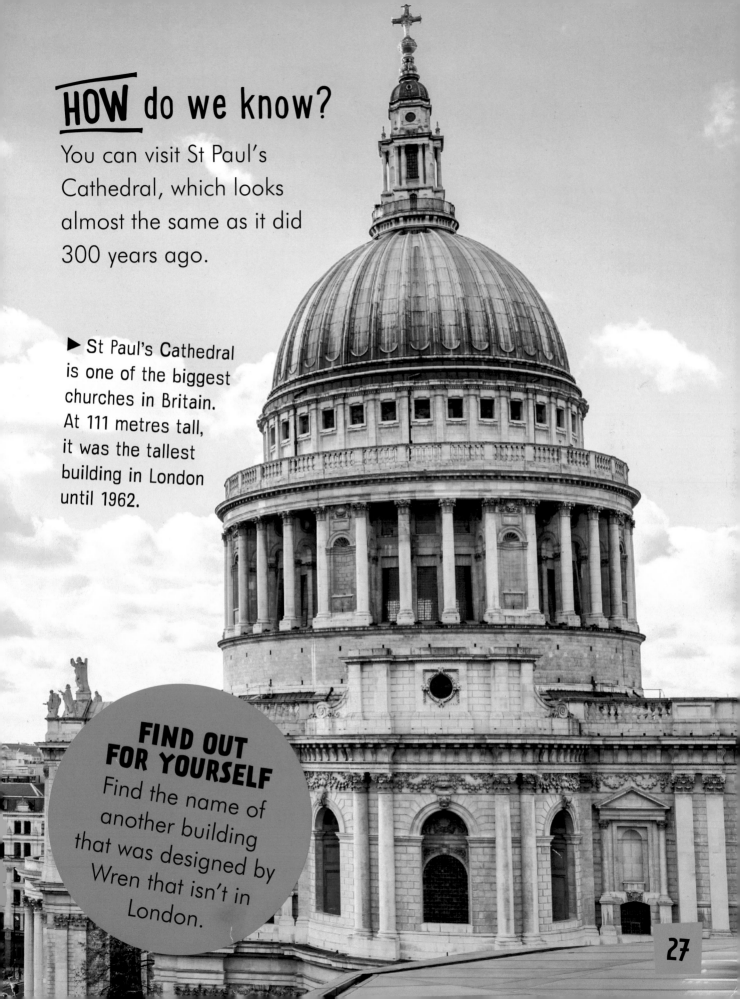

<u>HOW</u> do we know?

You can visit St Paul's Cathedral, which looks almost the same as it did 300 years ago.

▶ St Paul's Cathedral is one of the biggest churches in Britain. At 111 metres tall, it was the tallest building in London until 1962.

FIND OUT FOR YOURSELF
Find the name of another building that was designed by Wren that isn't in London.

REMEMBERING THE <u>FIRE</u>

As part of the rebuilding of London, a large stone **column** named the Monument was built close to Pudding Lane. The Monument was a way to celebrate the new buildings in London, while remembering the terrible events of the Great Fire.

Christopher Wren and the architect Robert Hooke (1635–1703) designed the Monument. It was completed in 1677 and still stands today, over 300 years later!

► The Monument

◄ The top of the Monument looks like flames.

FIND OUT FOR YOURSELF
How tall is the Monument?

HOW do we know?

You can visit the Monument in London. From the top of the Monument, you can see buildings that were rebuilt after the Great Fire, such as St Paul's Cathedral, and modern buildings.

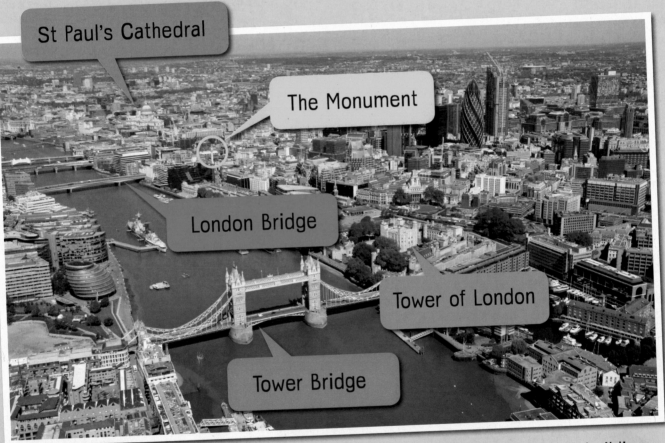

St Paul's Cathedral

The Monument

London Bridge

Tower of London

Tower Bridge

▲ Today, modern buildings surround the Monument.

WHAT do you think?

Have you visited any other monuments that were built in memory of an event or a person? Do you think that the Monument is a good way of remembering the Great Fire of London?

GLOSSARY

17th century – the period of time between 1600 and 1699

archaeologist – someone who looks for and studies objects from the past

architect – someone who designs buildings

ash – the grey powder that is left behind when something has been burnt

column – a tall post

damage – to harm or break something

destroy – to damage something so badly that it doesn't exist anymore

eyewitness – someone who sees an event happen

fire hook – a metal pole that was used to pull down walls

government – the group of people who control a country

gunpowder – a powder that explodes when you set it on fire

landscape – the way that an area looks

natural disaster – a natural event that causes a lot of damage, such as a flood or an earthquake

plague – a terrible disease that killed a lot of people in the past

possession – something that you own

record – information that is written down

rubble – broken pieces of a building

shore – the area of land next to water

spread – to move over a bigger and bigger area

talented – describes someone who is very good at doing something

valuable – something that is important to someone because it is worth a lot of money, or because the person loves it

TIMELINE

1665 — Over 100,000 people die from the plague in London.

2 Sept 1666 — A fire starts at a bakery in Pudding Lane, London.

3 Sept 1666 — A strong wind blows the fire across the centre of London. People escape the city with their possessions.

4 Sept 1666 — The fire continues to move across London. It doesn't manage to cross from the north side of the river to the south side.

5 Sept 1666 — The wind drops and the fire begins to die down.

6 Sept 1666 — The fire is finally put out. 13,000 buildings have been destroyed.

1667 — King Charles II makes new rules about buildings.

1677 — The Monument to the Great Fire of London is completed.

1711 — After 36 years, the rebuilding of St Paul's Cathedral is finished.

FIND OUT FOR YOURSELF ANSWERS

p7 – One. p11 – Thomas Farriner. p13 – 1660. p17 – Parmesan. p27 – Some buildings include the Sheldonian Theatre in Oxford and the Wren Library in Cambridge. p28 – 62 metres.

INDEX